FATIMA:

FATIMA:

Passion's Glory

TONY D. FLASH

Flash Supplements LLC

CONTENTS

COPY RIGHTS

FATIMA: Passion's Glory | Copyright © 2021 by Tony D. Flash

All rights reserved. No part of this publication may be reproduced, distributed, or transmitted in any form or by any means, including photocopying, recording, or other electronic or mechanical methods, without the prior written permission of the publisher, except in the case of brief quotations embodied in critical reviews and certain other non-commercial uses permitted by copyright law. For permission requests, contact the publisher, addressed "Attention: Permissions Coordinator," at the address below.

info@flashsupplementsllc.com @tonydflash @flashsupplementsllc

FIRST EDITION 2021 Written by: Tony D. Flash

Cover Design by Erin Babb

Editing, Text Layout, & Formatting by Cheyanne K. Gonzalez Photos by www.unsplash.com

Category: Poetry, Love, Physics, Trust, Change,

Printed in the (United States) by: (Ingram Spark)

The rain is a symbol of another chance it feed the earth. It's feed us all. My appreciation of the rain came earlier in life when I met this woman that taught me how to love the rain. She taught me that life was much more simple than what we make it. Even though she explained the ups and downs we would face she said complexity is the norm when a perspective is clustered with fear of what might be, "live for today even if you plan for tomorrow, be free" ... I wouldn't of been able to reach this frequency without that help... without that truth. I'm more grateful for the rain than I've ever been in my life. The rain is a second chance it's a metaphorical and physical symbol of nourishment, freedom, and opportunity. Every rain drop is different and every rain drop falls in a different spot but it rains around the world.

To be a drop of rain is to be free! To love the rain is to be pure that woman was pure. I named the book Fatima because it is believed to have extraordinary characteristics that can protect people from evil and other dangers not only does that name mean that but it' stands for the mother of all. Nature is the mother of all ....

My interpretation of what Fatima means is To be free of all limitations.

CHAPTER 1

She Taught Me

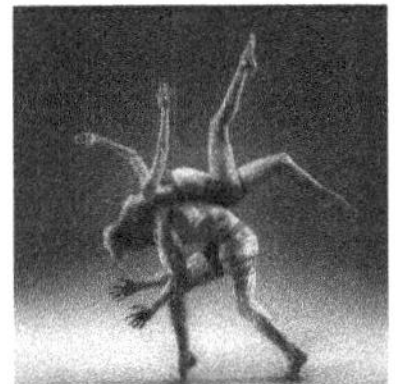

She taught me how to love the rain, It ain't been the same walking through the storm going through my brain. You loved me for the me I was then. You loved me for the me I am today. You saw the future in me and the future of me! When I cried apart of you died.....I didn't realize I was committing suicide. I assisted in the genocide of the ride or die! How could I! Equality is dead inequality is ahead Stupid boy use your head.. stupid boy chose the led ... to be mislead of course. You was right they wasn't for me, it's no ego here this isn't for me, choosing freedom here this far me! I dug a grave now I lay in it while water from the rain stays in it. Flooded with my intentions I can't stray from it. The weight of my actions .... Shit ain't no weighing it. She taught me how to love the rain ..... now I stay in it. The beauty of life is based off one's perspective, there is always good even if we define situations as bad. There is always light even in the dark. Sincerely the man who learned to love the rain.

CHAPTER 2

Dysmorphia

Down to the way you walk is my influence, I'm not a narcissistic, your love is Truant
My success in vein, abused because my love is fluent. "impudence" the discrepancies of a blocked eye! Eye cannot catch why the love is vague. Orchestration of the truth Is not desired so they yell love is pain. Tellers of untruths why? To control our brain?
I cannot salute the lack of tame. Losing yourself is toxic game.

CHAPTER 3

Lucid Dreamer

We commit perjurer instead of one another saying you can learn from me. A society that chooses to steal that's third degree. We damage or kill the life we steal... more like burglary. We dance in flames we are the perpetrators of our own fire! Arsonist of our own futures! We watch the smoke go up in the air and question the Ash. Most people begin to ebb with no water. Even though the soul say no farther. Detestation of what we chose, it wasn't chosen over night!

CHAPTER 4

The Galaxy

I'm scared to tell you that I love you and I need you. I'll sound the same like everyone else.... But this is different,....... I didn't love myself and I gave us less. I don't know the new you but I yearn for the true you. A shooting star in the distance that I hope to reach one day. Im not making a wish I rather travel past eclipses and enjoy the universe with you. Sit on top of the moon and watch the sun, I would say rotate around the world but what's the fun? Question everything! See it for what it is a flat plain, Level things! Pondering the escape from a past that doesn't own me. The cycle continues, the cycle continues... learn your gift after it's lost! Learn to love after the cost. Learn life after the closeness of death.

I'm on this quest, but it never felt right without you. I learned the moon and the stars never meant anything without my everything! To gaze upon life forces so strong I need my vision. The galaxy isn't a galaxy without us and it could never be them!

CHAPTER 5

Hypothetically

Covid doesn't exist we kiss and we aren't afraid to die. Hunger is no longer a issue because we chose to rise. Pollution was in the air but we traded that for Love now Love is in the air and that was our best solution. There's no prejudice around so now it's no more body's being found. Them little kids aren't being sold so those mothers don't have to frown. Trigger happy doesn't even exist! "Accidents" that changed our hearts now gone in the mist. Unbelievable scenes of jubilation cross our minds, look at the times! Joys around so no one could be down, we growing crops and eating from grapevines. My neighbor not depicted by the over reach of their ancestors, colors no longer matter! There is no split in culture we are all one. The ocean is so clean you could see the bottom. Genocide never existed so there's no wounds to heal...... doctors are free because care is real. Hypothetically speaking .... Love is the cure .....

CHAPTER 6

Reparations

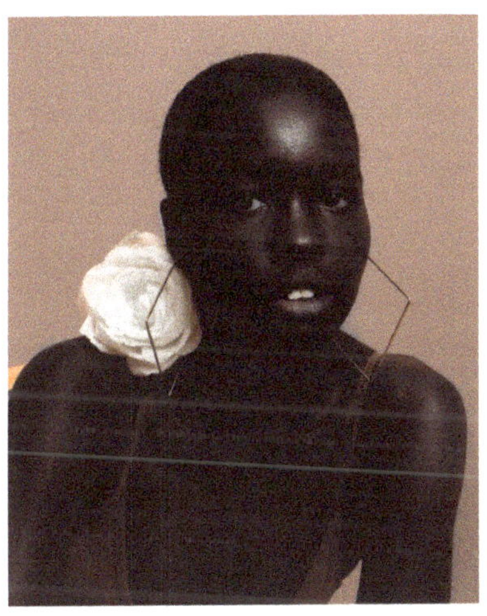

Give me a moment black woman to explain what I should and shouldn't. Let me tell you my wonders and why I couldn't,
I owe reparations Not just full paid vacations! My vacancy spiritually leaves you with physical emptiness, the reason your trust is lost ....
I haven't been here for a while it's no denial
I haven't been here for thyself. I won't blame the system, a

system isn't a system without my help. Difficult times our entire existence!

Not once did you quit us! Continued to raise us! Continue to birth us! Reparations of my absence isn't enough! Give me a moment black woman to explain what I should and shouldn't! The only woman who never questioned my blackness! The only woman who didn't have to grow to love the dark.

I'm sorry on my watch I let us fall apart!

Give me a moment black woman as I kneel down to pick up the pieces. I know I can't put it back together but understand I will never ever turn my back on another black woman! I will never be vacant these are your true reparations!

CHAPTER 7

Eye Don't Know

Anxiety represents my consciousness expressing myself after all this time, take a look inside you'll see my soul coruscate in the temple of my mind. Malcom X on repeat! By any means necessary! Bow to my feet for my enemy's necessary! Learn on repeat consistency ain't temporary. We learn to deceit that's the enemy's weaponry! Idk that's a true statement. I exposed the roots in nine acquire a knowledge of truth less lies
who despise? No one for course!
Accountability is the main itinerary. Trust the process and not the source!

CHAPTER 8

Just look

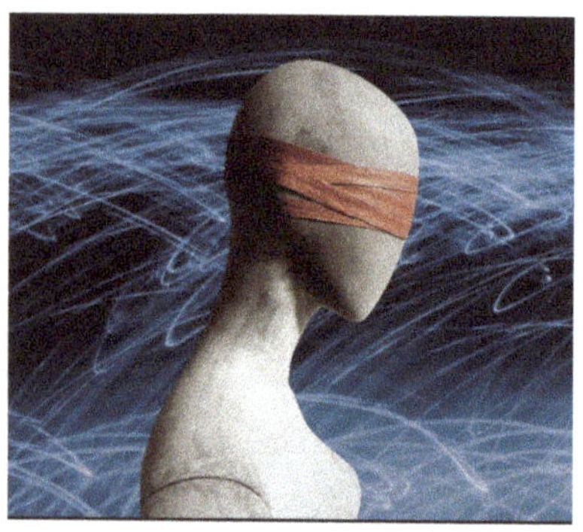

This is my encephalon in this one dimensional location. The light behind the picture gyrates through my darkest times. Absorbed what's left of me leaving me blindfolded in a trance like a manikin this is life! You have to believe in your path in order to achieve your destiny. Just look !

Nine

V=P-O / Vitality = Power - Obstruction

Nine when it comes to my soul even if we spend eternity learning. Three for all things that are me and for things that are not I am them! Oneness with duality purposely leading Nature. Six because the human race needs it! We choose to feed the opposite no explanation raging my soul is craving eliminate or dismantle the fake is fading. Maktub true freedoms for the taking. Around the corner twelve is waiting lurking and plotting because thirteen, thirteen that's a statement!

Reference = spiritual numbers

Jail

Jail is a vague word. It' doesn't truly explain
Domesticated beings of light. Revolving doors due to closed
minds that's probably their biggest fights. Mistakes turn into
felonies and felonies occupy the space that was once empty.
Shortage of time that doesn't exist until you sit still then every
second becomes a minute and every minute becomes an hour.
Oppression, depression, suicide, it all starts to look the same.

Ethnicity become's the topic of conversation because they've turned against each other now everyone is called out of their name. They don't realize we let our people down we loss, we aren't the ones around. It's ironic to be judged by 12 there innocence is paraded in front! Their faults hidden in the back. Jail ... it's just a building meant to dim the light. What about programs to educate the wrong on the right? They say that's there already but where's the change we ready. It's deeper than just hoping that a person will be alright. Imagine being thrown into a dark hole because you fought for your life. Jail domesticated beings of light!

CHAPTER 11

Breaking Toxic

Toxicity it starts within! Hey little woman this ain't a battle we gotta fight! Hey little woman we have child hood traumas we haven't healed. Hey little woman we can't allow toxic to lead. Love yourself in order to Nourish your soul. Hey little woman don't be afraid I promise you that this knowledge of self is gold. Hey little man it's okay to cry hey little man it's okay to ask why, hey little man don't let that anger take you. Hey little man there's no reason to lie. Hey little man always respect the little woman. Hey little man I understand that toxicity is taught through generations of misguided education and when you cross that point of change don't be afraid to stand. Hey little woman and little man breaking toxicity takes a life time!

CHAPTER 12

The Innocent Incarcerated Mind

I'm in the box some people call it the hole. It's feel like December I don't know to be frank. I do know I've been in here for 39 days I kept count by scratching lines into the wall. I'm starting to lose sanity. It's feeling more and more like insanity. My heartache's my body numb. I wanna move but it's so cold I rather keep the warmth in. It's just enough heat so I don't transition to the other side. "Orange suits" white stripes they slaved us before the box. I worked hard, I worked all night. I swear I tear! My feet are swollen. My back is done; that's just a modern day slavery! If you know what I mean I hope you can relate. To me! We call them Pataky's but they're converses with no comfort pain is unbearable. They might as well put a whip to our backs were trapped hoping we get release and they hoping we come back. I was innocent I just couldn't afford to fight back! I should kill "em all that's violent right? They took away my innocence. I'm innocent... every one screaming the same my vocals left unheard so I scream! They shout back you aren't in the right frame of mind. But I'm innocent!

CHAPTER 13

The Spirit D.O.B

You're only born once! Fabricated Illusions make life a mystery. We made titles, I think that's behind our misery! We titled sequences of change then we turn that into agony. My Epiphany gave me awareness that this is a trilogy. Divided among the less spiritually, in the confusion we made our own Caskets. Buried the disaster and pain grew instead! We have to make headway. I was born once but I'm leaving out the "dead way". So I choose to live in my rebirth. Demur I am to me! living once born in this realm conceive from just one. Clearance came back life is on sale don't miss out or you won't make bail! Trapped in the wonderful world that we all hail.... The physical realm where life and death is titled end and beginning.

CHAPTER 14

Let Me In

Let me be your asset I would never be your liability.
 Let me love you endlessly, boundlessly dancing with our spirits but still feeling corporeality obsessed with human nature Using physics to change our reality.

Heavier the density even without physical weight on my shoulders,

What I wanna be is your man abysmally in a paradox revisiting our Best memories, over and over what I can't be is your friend continuously thinking it's over

Loving you forever seems like a limitation. Hugging you forever seems like an invitation. Understanding my feelings have no constraint's. Lurking through my desperation I need you to hear me! What I wanna be is with you.

CHAPTER 15

The Regretful Man

When I speak to you I have feelings that want to burst out. I have things I wanna say. So much anxiety! it's anxiety to feel so deep for someone! It's a anxiety because nothing you could say or do could change my passion. It's anxiety because I've never felt so vulnerable! I know time changes things.... But the soul doesn't know time...

The soul is everlasting! The heart has to grow so when it breaks it repairs itself. Never the same as it was before. Growth is lessons and lessons is experience! The soul is forever ...this is forever anxiety that can't be fixed until my desire comes true....what I did to you ... Leave her alone she deserves better and I'm not better.... Kick the puddle after the water is spilled so she runs far away from me. Scream so she is afraid of me. Yell and fight so she doesn't think the same of me..... a coward at his best It's so strange to me.

CHAPTER 16

Blind

Even if you changed I'm in love with your soul. I'm in love with the change I haven't experienced I'm insane for being in love after all this change... I never knew what love was until I trusted the love I have for you not knowing the end of the road. Then it hit me love is faith. Faith is like walking on a frozen lake, we can only hope that it will never break swirling gust of winds take me for a spin like musical notes coming from an old violin. while I search for my twin flame I declare love, I declare purity. Blinded by my own ego

Preserved by own hate.....self sabotaging actions and still confused by their reactions!

Maybe I'm just acting? Fact is loving you is a fraction! Being in love with you makes me ecstatic. The road is enigmatic but I'm still strolling on blind faith! Blind I am with faith I stand! reflect on my options wishing I chose to be your man. Even though you might of changed I can see the pain! let me help you heal I can feel the rain! This is not regret But I hesitate what was once one is now a separate.

CHAPTER 17

The Consequences Of My Actions

Day after day we argue it's kills me inside to see what was once great turn into nothing my eyes red like in between east Africa coast and the Saudi Arabian peninsula. We past the point of no return, yet I cease fire and still go back for the love that I once knew. I started this war it just ended with you! Casualties .... I never fathomed.

Cruelly decided our fates acting like you aren't the one that made the best decisions. I'm at fault for it! No discussions you took the fall for it. You knew Eye couldn't understand I wasn't a real man and in your definition that was just me maintaining true. True to us, true to you, true to me. Contemplating our last good bye's instead of stopping to hear your cries. Now I meditate just so I can go back... but I can't go back ... the consequences of my actions.

The Rain

If i didn't love the rain I couldn't take a hike
If I didn't love the rain a puddle would be disastrous for me
If I didn't love the rain a river wouldn't be a view If I didn't love
the rain the sound of the drops couldn't come thru
Each drop of the rain Has it's own story
Each drop of rain has its own glory
Each drop of rain washes the pain
The shower from the sky if I didn't love the rain I wouldn't of
looked at the sky the same
If I didn't love the rain I wouldn't of understood the cycle
of life ....

CHAPTER 19

The Fallen

I've fallen from my grace! Fighting over race, judgmental is my fate. Hoping I'm not to late. Realizing what I hate! Destruction of our faith! Wait.... The seed was planted long before me. I took for granted what's before me. I leave a pattern of madness... they might follow the sadness. I go deeper in the trenches of hysteria ... Eye come out not even recognizing who I am, the blank stare at a face in the mirror wondering what I am! The journey is deep I can't sleep walking for days the sun on my feet! It's getting brighter my eyes lowering.... My eyes closed .... It's open ... I'm still moving. I feel better, I think better I realize .....He who is she carried me off the path I was taking. Now I see the point of clarity We are human variations.

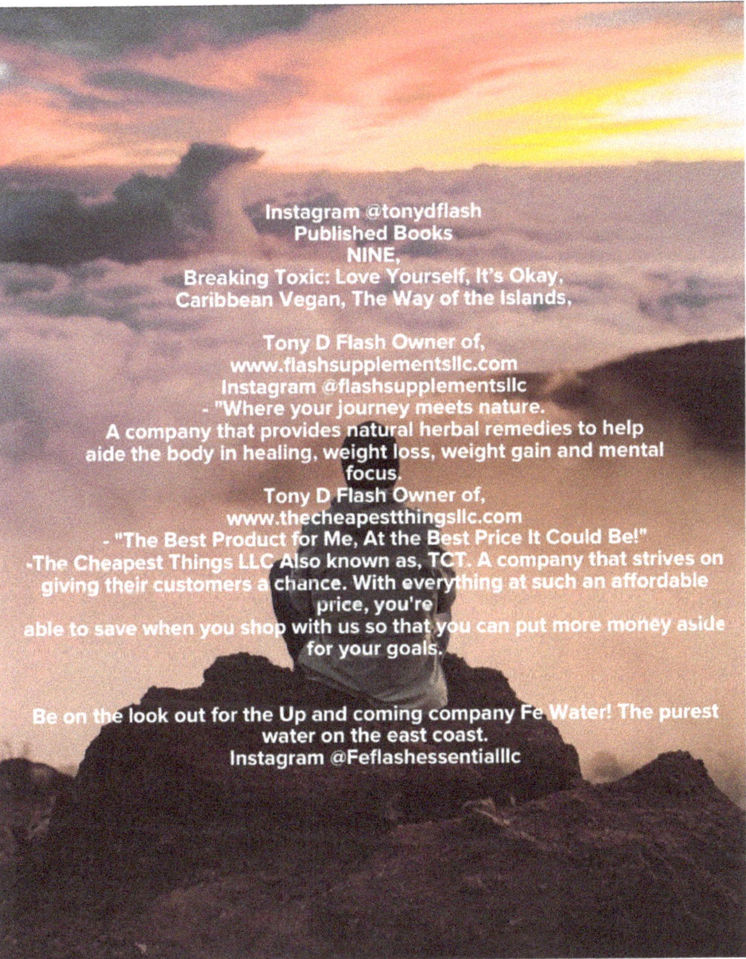

Instagram @tonydflash
Published Books
NINE,
Breaking Toxic: Love Yourself, It's Okay,
Caribbean Vegan, The Way of the Islands,

Tony D Flash Owner of,
www.flashsupplementsllc.com
Instagram @flashsupplementsllc
- "Where your journey meets nature.
A company that provides natural herbal remedies to help
aide the body in healing, weight loss, weight gain and mental
focus.
Tony D Flash Owner of,
www.thecheapestthingsllc.com
- "The Best Product for Me, At the Best Price It Could Be!"
-The Cheapest Things LLC Also known as, TCT. A company that strives on
giving their customers a chance. With everything at such an affordable
price, you're
able to save when you shop with us so that you can put more money aside
for your goals.

Be on the look out for the Up and coming company Fe Water! The purest
water on the east coast.
Instagram @Feflashessentialllc